This or That

Questions
About the
Human Body

You Decide!

by Kathryn Clay

CAPSTONE PRESS
a capstone imprint

Capstone Captivate is published by Capstone Press, an imprint of Capstone.
1710 Roe Crest Drive
North Mankato, Minnesota 56003
www.capstonepub.com

**Library of Congress Cataloging-in-Publication Data is available on the Library
of Congress website.**
ISBN: 978-1-4966-9537-6 (library binding)
ISBN: 978-1-4966-9698-4 (paperback)
ISBN: 978-1-9771-5513-9 (eBook PDF)

Summary: Presents intriguing questions and information related to the human
body and prompts readers to pick one choice or the other.

Image Credits
iStockphoto: jxfzsy, 18, Maartje van Caspel, 20; Shutterstock: 3445128471, cover
top left, Africa Studio, 29, Andrew Angelov, 21, Arlene Gapusan, 16, CGN089, 24,
Chirtsova Natalia, 19, deepadesigns, design element, Denis Kuvaev, 17, Duplass, 23,
Elizaveta Galitckaia, 15, ESB Professional, 14, GaudiLab, 8, Goldencow Images, 6,
GoodStudio, design element, guraydere, 9, Jetsadaphoto, 7, Jihan Nafiaa Zahri, 10,
Kateryna Kon, cover bottom right, Life_imageS, 11, Master1305, 25, MDGRPHCS,
cover bottom left, Monkey Business Images, 4–5, oneinchpunch, 26, SciePro, 3,
Stefano Garau, 28, udeyismail, 27, Vadiar, 22, VaLiza, 13, WAYHOME studio, 12

Editorial Credits
Editors: Michelle Parkin and Carrie Sheely; Designer: Sarah Bennett; Media
Researcher: Tracy Cummins; Production Specialist: Spencer Rosio

All internet sites appearing in back matter were available and accurate when this
book was sent to press.

Words in **bold** are in the glossary.

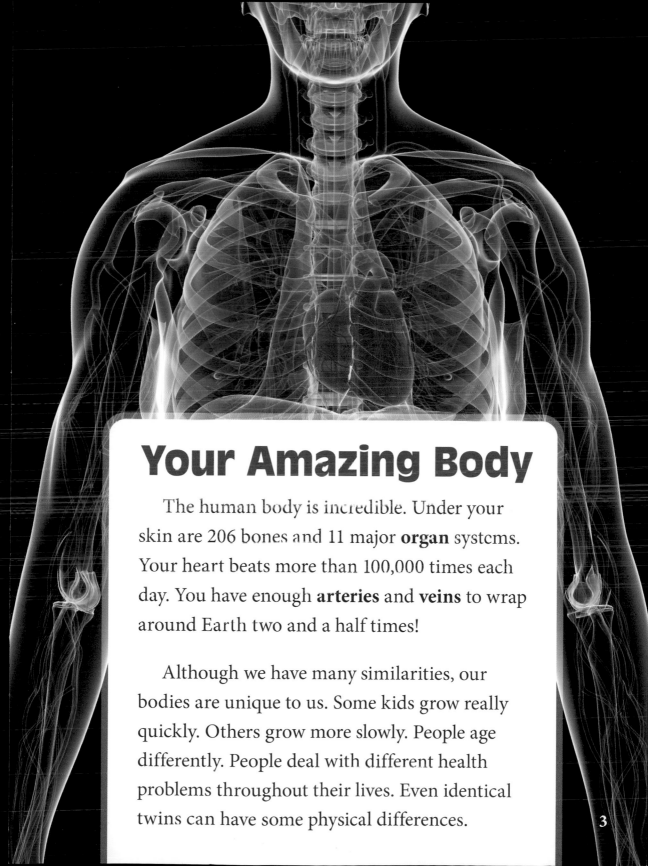

Your Amazing Body

The human body is incredible. Under your skin are 206 bones and 11 major **organ** systems. Your heart beats more than 100,000 times each day. You have enough **arteries** and **veins** to wrap around Earth two and a half times!

Although we have many similarities, our bodies are unique to us. Some kids grow really quickly. Others grow more slowly. People age differently. People deal with different health problems throughout their lives. Even identical twins can have some physical differences.

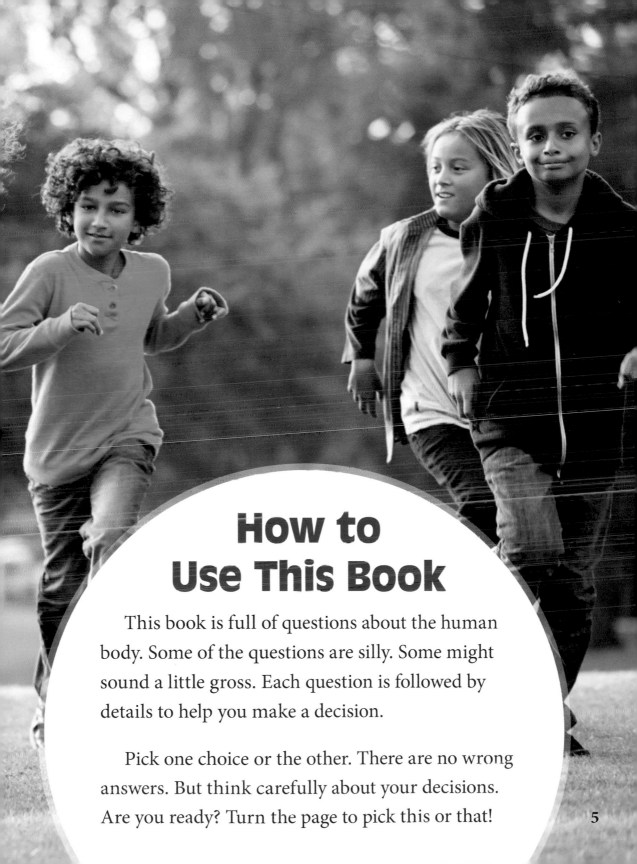

How to Use This Book

This book is full of questions about the human body. Some of the questions are silly. Some might sound a little gross. Each question is followed by details to help you make a decision.

Pick one choice or the other. There are no wrong answers. But think carefully about your decisions. Are you ready? Turn the page to pick this or that!

✓ can change hair styles quickly

✓ use a lot of shampoo and other hair products

✓ could have long leg and arm hair

The hair on your head grows an average of 0.5 inches (1.3 centimeters) each month. But what if it grew twice as fast—or more? It might sound fun to quickly go from a short do to long locks. However, the extra costs of shampoo and haircuts would add up fast. And don't forget about the hair on your legs and arms. Speedy hair growth might leave you covered in thick hair!

✓ good for scratching itches

✓ bacteria bonanza

✓ hard to grab things

Long nails might be great for scratching an itch. But they come with a cost. Lots of **bacteria** live under your nails. The longer the nails, the more room for bacteria. The bacteria can cause infections. **Fungus** can grow there too. Long nails might make it hard to type or grab things. You could be constantly clipping your nails.

✔ eyes like an eagle

✔ other senses wouldn't be as strong

✔ wouldn't be able to read books

Good long-distance vision allows eagles to see animals they hunt from the sky. For us, that would be like seeing a tiny ant from a tall building. But your brain would use a lot of energy to see, so other senses wouldn't work as well. It would be harder to smell or taste. You wouldn't be able to read books. And you'd have to watch TV from across the street!

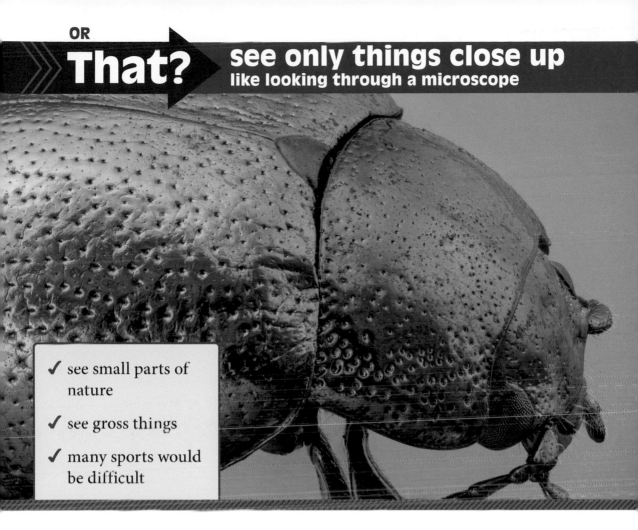

- ✓ see small parts of nature
- ✓ see gross things
- ✓ many sports would be difficult

With a microscope, you can see tiny things that otherwise wouldn't be visible to the human eye. You could zoom in on a bug or a leaf. But having microscopic vision might not be so fun. **Microbes** such as bacteria and **mites** live on your skin. Some microbes gobble up your dead skin. Imagine seeing billions of them all over you! And playing many sports would be hard or impossible. You wouldn't be able to see where to aim a ball!

This → to have everything smell like farts

✔ unpleasant smell

✔ miss out on many other smells

✔ might affect sense of taste

The average person farts 10 to 20 times each day. Nearly 99 percent of farts don't smell. But the remaining 1 percent can be very unpleasant. If everything smelled like terrible toots, you might feel sick. You'd miss out on the nearly 1 trillion different smells humans can detect. And nearly 80 percent of our sense of taste is related to smell. How good would a warm cookie taste if it smelled like a fart?

- ✔ miss out on other flavors
- ✔ eating food not as enjoyable
- ✔ might not know if food is spoiled

People are born with 10,000 taste buds. Taste buds recognize five specific tastes—salty, sweet, bitter, **umami**, and sour. If you could taste only sour things, you'd miss out on so many flavors. Eating food wouldn't be as enjoyable. You wouldn't be able to tell if the food you're eating is spoiled. This could lead to food poisoning. Symptoms include stomach pain, vomiting, and diarrhea.

- ✓ lots of bacteria
- ✓ can get E. coli or shigella infections
- ✓ infections can cause severe illness

Dipping your toothbrush into the toilet is a bad idea. Every gram of human poop has billions of bacteria. Some of these bacteria will be in the toilet water. The bacteria can include E. coli and shigella. People who are infected with these bacteria can get diarrhea and have stomach cramps. You can also get staph infections, which can be serious.

✔ stinky smell

✔ chunky

✔ can cause food poisoning

Have you ever opened a container of milk and smelled something stinky? Your sense of smell is telling you that your milk has spoiled. Milk spoils from bacteria growth. In addition to the smell, spoiled milk often turns yellow and chunky. Drinking it can cause food poisoning.

✔ ace tests

✔ be terrific at trivia

✔ remember bad memories

Your brain is like a computer. You put in data, and your brain retrieves the information. We can remember many sights, smells, sounds, and feelings. But people can recall only some memories. As we age, this process gets harder. Imagine remembering everything you've ever seen or heard. You'd ace all your tests at school. You'd be a trivia star. But you also would recall any bad memories.

- ✓ swim without weight of air tank
- ✓ watch sea life
- ✓ might have some health benefits

Most people can hold their breath for up to two minutes. Imagine being able to hold your breath for hours! You'd be able to swim underwater all day without an oxygen tank. You could take your time studying sea animals and plants. Scientists think holding your breath can even have some health benefits. It might be able to keep **cells** healthy and prevent bacterial infections.

✔ could give you superhero-like status

✔ use it or lose it

✔ could accidentally hurt people

The body has more than 600 muscles. They connect to the skeleton. Muscles pull bones to move the body. With mighty muscles, you could be like a superhero! But you'd have to work your muscles regularly to keep them strong. Controlling your power would be tough too. If you weren't careful, a friendly handshake could become a bone crusher!

✓ get places fast

✓ need to eat a lot

✓ can lead to injuries

Zip over to a friend's house. Never be late again! Running at super speeds would come in handy! Running is also great exercise. It strengthens the heart and lungs. But muscles use a lot of energy as you run. You'd have to eat often to refuel. And doing the same motion over and over again may lead to leg injuries.

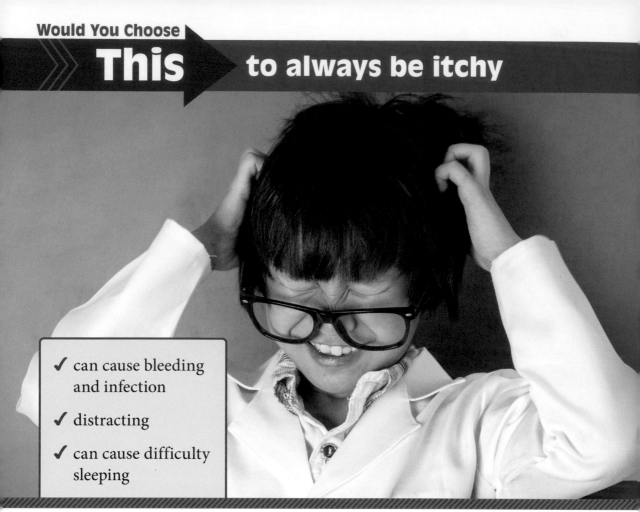

✔ can cause bleeding and infection

✔ distracting

✔ can cause difficulty sleeping

Many things can cause your skin to feel itchy, including rashes, dry skin, and mosquito bites. Scratching too much can cause your skin to bleed or become infected. It could be distracting when you are trying to focus. All that itching can keep you from a restful sleep too.

✓ distracting

✓ can spread sicknesses

✓ need to cover coughs

Germs such as **viruses** can cause coughs. Coughing is your body's way of removing **mucus** or other things that are stuck in or irritating your airway. It produces air that blasts out of your mouth. If you coughed constantly, it would be harder to breathe normally while exercising. It would also be distracting and make sleeping difficult. You'd need to cover your coughs. Coughs can spread germs and get others sick.

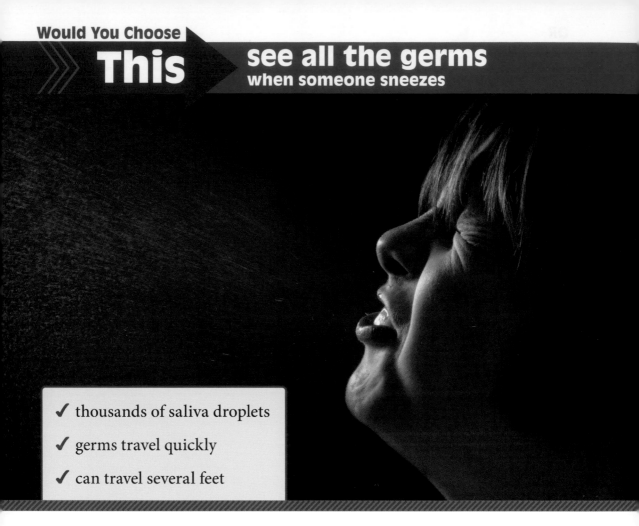

✔ thousands of saliva droplets

✔ germs travel quickly

✔ can travel several feet

When someone sneezes, thousands of saliva droplets shoot out. Many health experts believe the droplets can travel at least 100 miles (322 kilometers) per hour! Each droplet is filled with germs. Imagine watching those germs travel 8 feet (2.4 meters) or more! It's important to cover your sneezes.

✔ hands are germ magnets

✔ germs can infect others

✔ could lead to constant handwashing

Our hands are covered with germs. Imagine seeing every single one! Germs get on your hands as you touch objects. They can then transfer from person to person. The germs can get into our eyes, noses, and mouths, causing sicknesses. People's hands spread up to 80 percent of illness-causing germs. Seeing all those germs might cause you to wash your hands—a lot!

✔ more time to do activities you enjoy

✔ no longer have nightmares

✔ no longer have good dreams

People spend almost a third of their lives sleeping. Sleep is a time for the body to rest and repair. Without enough, you become grumpy. You can't focus. But what if you could be fine without sleep? You'd have tons of free time! You could say goodbye to nightmares. But you'd have to say so long to good dreams too.

- ✓ won't feel hungry
- ✓ miss out on foods you like
- ✓ might feel left out

Food gives the body nutrients that keep us healthy. Not needing to eat would have its benefits. You'd never feel hungry. Imagine, though, never enjoying your favorite dessert again. You also might feel left out when family and friends eat together.

- ✔ fall often
- ✔ more injuries
- ✔ miss out on many activities

Picture a baby learning to walk. The baby is unsteady and falls often. That's probably how you'd look with poor balance. A lack of balance would increase your risk of getting hurt. It could make you feel dizzy and have blurry vision. And you can forget about riding a bike or skating!

✓ strained muscles and joints

✓ more aches and pains

✓ increased risk of severe injuries

Flexibility means being able to bend, twist, and stretch easily. It reduces your risk of getting hurt when playing sports. With poor flexibility, your muscles and joints would be strained. Your muscles would tire more easily. More aches and pains would be likely. Severe injuries such as **ligament** tears could be more likely to happen too.

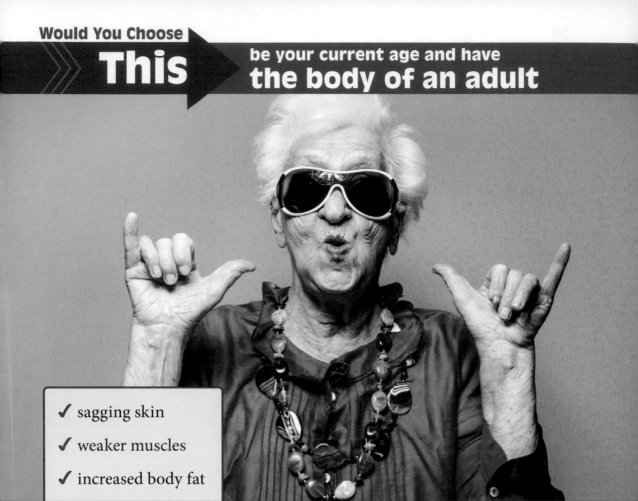

- ✓ sagging skin
- ✓ weaker muscles
- ✓ increased body fat

It might be fun to look like an adult. But being older comes with some problems. Our bodies experience wear and tear as we age. Skin can sag and wrinkle. Muscles weaken. Stiff joints can make moving more difficult. Body fat increases. This can put people at risk for serious diseases such as **diabetes**.

OR
That?
**be your current age and have
the body of a baby**

- ✓ flexible bones
- ✓ poor eyesight
- ✓ small stomach

Babies' bodies are different from those of adults. Babies have more flexible bones. This would protect you from breaking bones. But newborns are only able to see well 8 to 12 inches (20 to 30 cm) in front of their faces. Everything beyond that is a blur! Another downside? A baby's stomach is only about the size of an egg. You can forget about eating a slice of pizza!

This → have eyes that change color based on **your emotions**

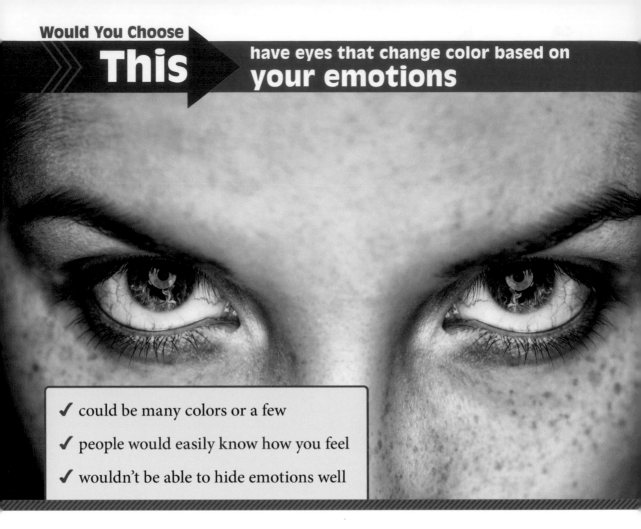

- ✓ could be many colors or a few
- ✓ people would easily know how you feel
- ✓ wouldn't be able to hide emotions well

Some scientists say humans have only four basic emotions. They are happiness, sadness, fear, and anger. Others say we have 34,000! Your eyes might be a rainbow of colors. With color-changing eyes, people would always know how you're feeling. Your eyes might give away what you are feeling when you are trying to hide an emotion. It could be hard to keep a surprise birthday party a secret from your friend!

- ✓ constant color switches
- ✓ wouldn't need to dye hair
- ✓ people might use you to get weather information

With hair that changes color based on the outdoor temperature, you wouldn't need to dye your hair. It would be constantly changing colors. But you wouldn't get to choose the colors. And it might be annoying if people treated you like a human thermometer!

Lightning Round
Would you choose to . . .

➥ only be able to walk on all fours
or only be able to walk sideways?

➥ have super strong legs
or super strong arms?

➥ have burps that are extra loud
or extra stinky?

➥ be always cold
or always hot?

➥ be the fastest kid
or the smartest kid at school?

➥ have stinky armpits
or stinky feet?

➥ have a permanent fearful facial expression
or a surprised one?

➥ have eyes in the back of your head
or super hearing?

Glossary

artery (AR-tuh-ree)—a tube that carries blood away from the heart to all parts of the body

bacteria (bak-TEER-ee-uh)—microscopic living things that exist all around you and inside you; some bacteria cause diseases

cell (SEL)—a tiny structure that makes up all living things

diabetes (dy-uh-BEE-teez)—a disease in which there is too much sugar in the blood

fungus (FUHN-guhs)—a living thing similar to a plant, but without flowers, leaves, or green coloring

ligament (LIG-uh-muhnt)—a band of tissue that connects bones to bones

microbe (MYE-krobe)—a tiny living thing that is too small to be seen without a microscope

mite (MITE)—a tiny animal with eight legs that is related to the spider

mucus (MYOO-kuhss)—a slimy fluid that coats and protects the inside of your mouth, nose, and throat

organ (OR-guhn)—a part of the body that does a certain job; your heart, lungs, and kidneys are organs

umami (oo-MAH-mee)—a taste that has a rich or meaty flavor; cheese, cooked meat, mushrooms, and some vegetables have umami flavor

vein (VAYN)—a blood vessel that carries blood to the heart

virus (VYE-russ)—a germ that copies itself inside the body's cells; viruses can cause diseases

Read More

Abbott, Simon. *100 Questions About the Human Body.* White Plains, NY: Peter Pauper Press, 2019.

Bennett, Howard. *The Fantastic Body: What Makes You Tick & How You Get Sick.* Emmaus, PA: Rodale Kids, 2017.

Hutmacher, Kimberly M. *Your Nose Never Stops Growing and Other Cool Human Body Facts.* North Mankato, MN: Capstone Press, 2019.

Internet Sites

KidsHealth: What Are Taste Buds?
kidshealth.org/en/kids/taste-buds.html

Mocomi: Fun Facts About the Human Body
mocomi.com/human-body-facts/

National Geographic Kids: Weird but True!: Human Body 2
kids.nationalgeographic.com/explore/adventure_pass/weird-but-true/humanbody2/